ALL COLOR BOOK OF
GREEK MYTHOLOGY

BY RICHARD PATRICK
INTRODUCTION BY BARBARA LEONIE PICARD

OCTOPUS BOOKS
LONDON NEW YORK SYDNEY HONG KONG

First published 1972 by
Octopus Books Limited
59 Grosvenor Street, London W1

ISBN 7064 0123 9
Distributed in the USA by Crescent Books,
a Division of Crown Publishers, Inc.
© Octopus Books Limited
Filmset by Yendall & Co Limited
Produced by Mandarin Publishers
Printed in Hong Kong

CONTENTS

Introduction to
GREEK MYTHOLOGY

Since that stage in evolution when man ceased to be an animal and became *homo sapiens*, it has been inherent in his nature, on looking at the world about him with wondering and puzzled eyes, to ask the questions 'Why?' and 'How?' It is the results of his groping attempts throughout the ages to find the answer to these questions which we call religion—or mythology: for we are inclined to consider our own beliefs—if we have any—as religion, and other people's beliefs as mythology.

A myth then is firstly, man's attempt to explain the world and the things he sees in it, and to make intelligible to himself the natural phenomena which condition his way of life in that world. His beliefs will vary according to this way of life and its needs. For example, to nomadic herdsmen, wandering about and disputing grazing territory with rival tribes, a strong, belligerent sky-god will be the best protector; while to a peaceable and settled agricultural community it is the fruitfulness of the earth-mother which is all important.

Secondly, and at a later and somewhat higher stage of human culture, a myth seeks also to justify an established social pattern together with its traditions and ritual; and it records, as it were dramatically, the historical invasions and migrations, changes of leadership and foreign influences, which combined to establish that social pattern. This second type of myth will tend to produce a hierarchy of gods which parallels the society of its believers: for instance, the gods of ancient China were members of a divine bureaucracy resembling in almost all respects the political administration of their worshippers.

At some stage in the long, slow development of these two types of myth, there will come a priest-poet, often semi-legendary, who will rationalize his people's beliefs and give a formal shape to their myth, as did Homer and Hesiod for the Greeks, and in this manner is a national religion established. And later, much later, though still based on the same primitive beginnings, will come—as they did for the Romans—the elegant sophistications of an Ovid with his *Metamorphoses*, or of an Apuleius with his charming allegory of Cupid and Psyche.

The precise difference between a myth and a folk-tale has long vexed scholars, because in many examples the theme and content of both are similar enough for their stories to be in essence the same. Just where exactly do the traditions of a people cease to be myths and become merely folk-tales? It is now generally agreed that if a story tells of a happening which affects the whole world, or all the members of a certain community, and is set at a time before a pattern of everyday life has been established, it is a myth.

If, on the other hand, a similar happening affects an individual living in a roughly identifiable historical or modern age, and in a setting recognizable to the hearers of the story, then it is a folk-tale.

It therefore follows that myths tell stories of the beginnings of things, and concern mainly the gods and those semi-divine culture heroes who often stand for abstract qualities—courage, kingship, warrior's strength, and so on—while folk-tales tell of individual human beings and their personal adventures, and often of anthropomorphic animals and their doings. A myth explains and rationalizes and is, for those who believe it, perpetually and repeatedly true; a folk-tale seeks only to instruct and to entertain. Thus in Jewish tradition, Adam the First Man for whom a mate was created from one of his ribs, and the Welsh solar hero Lleu whose wife Blodeuwedd was formed for him from flowers by the magician Gwydion, are part, respectively, of the Jewish and Celtic mythologies. But Cinderella's prince, wandering the land with the glass slipper in search of a particular, once-glimpsed bride is the protagonist in a folk-tale.

The myths of the ancient Greeks can be divided into three groups; firstly, myths of the Olympian gods—that is of Zeus the father-god, and of the more important of his fellow-deities; secondly, myths which explain natural phenomena; and thirdly, the hero-myths which relate the deeds and adventures of mortal heroes who were often of semi-divine parentage or ancestry, and many of whom were later deified and became numbered amongst the lesser gods of the Greek pantheon.

Greek religion followed a usual pattern of development, progressing from the simple fertility rites practised by the individual either on his own behalf or on behalf of his family, to the established state-religion with its public festivals and formalized procedures. As it developed, it shed or altered some beliefs and encompassed and adapted others. Sometimes it seemed to advance along more enlightened paths, and at other times it seemed to fall back again into a more antiquated usage, with its attendant barbarities. Yet gradually those early barbarities will have been entirely suppressed or else superceded by rites more in keeping with a higher level of culture. Religious emphasis will have varied from locality to locality; sophisticated ritual evolved more fully in the cities and larger centres of communal life; while among the primitive country folk—such as in rural Arcadia—the old superstitions and crude practices will have persisted alongside simplifications of the newer, polished forms.

The history of the development of Greek worship may be said roughly to cover, like the Christian, around 2000 years; but unlike the Christian faith Greek religion had no clear cut body of dogma, no sacred and supposedly god-inspired writings of the nature of the Jewish and Christian Bible or the Islamic Koran, and no compulsory creed, binding upon its worshippers. And this is probably why it could put up so little resistance to the spread of

Christianity: its tolerance and its respect for the adaptations and the varieties of belief of the individual were its own downfall. To the Greeks the word *hairetikos*—heretic—meant 'able to choose' and had no derogatory implication. Admittedly one of the charges brought against Socrates amounted to that of blasphemy—but then Socrates' enemies were short of ammunition and in need of every weapon, however blunt, upon which they could lay their hands. The idea of any fanatical, suppressive and persecuting religious body in the nature of the Christian Holy Office would have been not merely repugnant, but unthinkable to the Greeks, one of whose best-known maxims was 'Nothing to excess'.

Except perhaps for the later, secret, mystery cults which spread to Greece from the East, Greek faith was primarily materialistic and practical. It was a religion of everyday life unconcerned with other worldliness and the Greeks knew their deities and the accepted attributes and appearance of those deities, not through any supposed mystical experience, but through poetry and art. Poets contradicted each other in their works, as did Homer and Hesiod in some respects and art changed its style from age to age and from place to place but to the Greeks all was acceptable.

It is generally presumed today that in the prehistoric European communities, as in those of Asia Minor, Syria and Libya, the organized worship of a mother-goddess preceded that of a father-god. Man might have been taller, stronger and swifter, but it was woman who was the awe-inspiring mystery, with her strange monthly cycles, corresponding to the cycles of the moon by which man first learnt to reckon time in periods of more than a single day; it was woman who suckled and reared the young of the tribe; and above all it was woman who, alone or by the grace of some unseen supernatural power, perpetuated the race. Granted that from the moment when man first discovered the all-important truth, namely, that a child, so far from being conceived parthenogenetically, or being sired by a spirit of the wind or the waters of a stream, needs a human father for its existence, then the supreme power of woman—and with it the supreme power of the goddess—began to decline. But it was to be many ages before the Great Goddess was forced to yield her foremost position to the father-god. And in the ancient world she was never entirely ousted, never relegated to a place of no importance. In Greece, the protector and patron of Athens, even at the height of its political and military glory was the goddess Athene; and even in historical times there were religious festivals exclusive to women, such as the Thesmophoria, celebrated in Attica during the month of October, from which men were forbidden—a situation which the dramatist Aristophanes, in his *Thesmophoriazusae* uses to such splendidly ribald comic advantage.

Early in the second millennium BC the Hellenic invasions of mainland Greece began. At first they will have been

on a small scale and far less destructive than those which followed them. These early so-called Aeolian and Ionian invasions were probably little more than the infiltration of armed bands of nomadic herdsmen who pressed southwards in search of a more settled existence. They probably spoke an early form of Indo-European language and worshipped the Aryan trinity of sky-gods, Indra, Varuna and Mitra. After initial skirmishes, they will no doubt have settled down peaceably enough and intermarried with the pre-Hellenic agricultural peoples whom they found in Thessaly and central Greece: and their gods will have been accepted by these goddess-worshipping farmers as new children of the Mother.

After the Aeolian and Ionian invasions the more destructive and far reaching Achaean and Dorian invasions as they are called came from the north. This time the invaders were larger bands of experienced warriors rather than herdsmen and peaceable settlement and intermarriage were less to their liking than conquest and appropriation of territory and the slaughter or enslavement of those whose lands they invaded. The initial uneasy relationship between conquering invaders and conquered native inhabitants, might still be observed unchanged in classical times in Sparta, where the pre-Dorian population had been entirely enslaved and formed the Helots, an unprivileged class which performed all menial tasks and was utterly subservient to the ruling warrior class, by whom it was never assimilated.

At a time when the Greek mainland was still in a state of barbarism, there was already a flourishing and mainly peaceable civilization on the island of Crete, with strong trade connections with the East and in particular with Egypt. This civilization is known as Minoan from the name of its legendary founder, King Minos. Around 1600 BC its influence spread to the mainland, having its strongest effect in Argolis, where it resulted in the so-called Mycenaean civilization, centred around the town of Mycenae. In about 1400 BC the Minoan civilization on Crete collapsed probably as the result of a natural disaster—an earthquake, or the eruption of a volcano—which was followed by a successful invasion from the mainland of a powerful army which took full advantage of the chaos and disorganization brought about by the recent disaster.

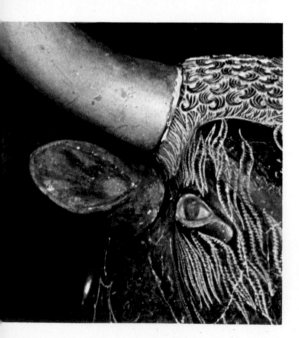

The history of the development of Greek religion shows it to have been influenced by beliefs from many other lands, including Babylonia, Egypt, Palestine and Phrygia but it is in Crete that its true beginnings are to be found. There, as elsewhere, the first forms of worship will have been the veneration of natural objects such as rocks, trees and animals; and of stylizations of certain man-made objects of vital importance to man's survival such as weapons, the hearth, a supporting roof-pillar and so on. The chief amongst these cult objects will have survived into the period of anthropomorphic deities to become attributes or symbols of the deities.

In Crete the special survivals were the Minoan doubleheaded axe, now well known from its many representations in Cretan art; the bull, a symbol of virility in several religions; the dove, a bird much given to mating–display and therefore associated with fertility; and the snake which periodically sloughs its skin and may from this be said to annually reborn. The snake in particular became much venerated in Greece in the classical period: and to this very day in certain country districts it is the subject of reverent superstition amongst the Greek peasants. Votive statuettes from shrines and tombs in Crete and depictions in art of these three creatures and of the doubleheaded axe are common, so also are the numerous representations of the Cretan Great Goddess in her several forms. Probably one of the best-known figurines from the ancient world is that statue of the so-called Minoan snake-goddess —the Great Goddess, or her priestess, dressed as a fashionable Cretan lady with bared breasts and flounced skirt, holding one of her sacred snakes in either hand.

Though something may be conjectured, we know little of the actual practices of Cretan religion or of its myths other than what has survived in an adapted form in later Hellenic practices. We do not even know the names of the Great Goddess, though one of them, in her aspect as Mother, was probably Rhea; and as the springtime Maiden she seems to have sometimes been called Britomartis. But under whatever names she was worshipped she will undoubtedly have been at first, all-powerful and revered throughout Crete in her three aspects as Maiden, Mother and Old Woman and she presided in one or other of her three forms, over every phase of human life and every occurrence in the daily round.

The pattern of annual worship in early Crete will probably have been similar to that offered to the Great Goddess in every place where she was supreme. She was represented by her high priestess, whose chosen consort was the father of the child which she bore annually—her fruitfulness being both the outward sign of the goodwill of the goddess towards the worshippers, and an encouraging reminder to the fields to give good yield that year, and to the flocks and herds to multiply. At first this consort will have been slain annually and replaced by a successor, probably at seed-sowing time when the sacrificed consort's blood and the pieces of his body will have been sprinkled and scattered on the fields to fertilize them.

From place to place the method will have varied by which the consort was slain: but on mainland Greece and in some localities of Asia Minor we can guess at it from clues given in myths concerning local deities and heroes who will, originally, have been consorts of the goddess. For instance, in Mysia the consort, like Hylas was drowned; in Thrace he was torn in pieces by the women worshippers or the priestesses, as was Orpheus; around Mount Ida in Asia Minor where the Great Goddess was worshipped as Cybele, we can tell that he was bled to death from the fate of Attis; and in Elis he was probably flung from a moving chariot, as was Oenomaus. We cannot be sure how he was slain in Crete, but perhaps he was despatched by means of the doubleheaded axe.

Gradually the position of the consort will have increased in importance. There will have been occasions during his year of office when, wearing the sacred robes of the goddess-priestess and temporarily invested with her magical power, he will have acted as her understudy. Also as time went on, it became the custom to kill each year not last year's consort, but a youth chosen in his place. And so from these adaptations and variations of earlier practice, will have arisen the first concept of kingship.

In Crete the Great Goddess's consort—the corn-youth, the priest-king, the dying-god—was from early times associated with the bull, an association which owed much to influence from the bull-cults of the East, such as those of Sumeria and Elam. Later, after the destruction of Minoan power, this Cretan bull-god was equated with Zeus, the sky-god from the mainland, and his attributes were assimilated with those of the newcomer. The fact that Zeus, supreme god of the Greek pantheon in later times, was originally a fusion of two important gods (for a moment we may here disregard the many minor, local mainland deities whose cults were swallowed up by his) is clearly displayed by the divergence of sites claimed as his birthplace. These sites include Arcadia, Messenia and Olympia—this last claim being made in a tradition which offers an explanation of the founding of the Olympic Games. But none of these mainland sites has the importance of Crete, from where comes a full and detailed version of the story of his birth as the son of Rhea—one of the Great Goddess's names as Mother. 'Cretan-born' was a stock epithet of Zeus. Moreover, if further proof is needed that Zeus, who became the immortal, never-aging, supreme god of historical times, was once the annually-dying consort of the Great Goddess, it is offered by the existence of the several sites revered as his burial-place, both on Crete—at Knossos and at Mount Dicte—and on the mainland.

After the fall of Crete, the leadership of the Aegean world passed to Mycenae in Argolis, where a culture very different from that of Crete had grown up over the years, though it had originally owed much to Cretan influence. Compared with Knossos, that splendid, largely unfortified Cretan city, with its peaceable, luxurious way of life and its pre-eminent Great Goddess, Mycenae was little more than a huge armed fortress of god-worshipping warriors, lead by a strong priest-king.

The power of the Great Goddess was now everywhere being superceded by the power of the god. But she did not surrender without a fight. Those myths which tell of the too-frequent quarrels between Zeus and Hera, his sister and queen, may appear undignified to us at first sight, but are simply allegories of the struggle between the old worship and the new—as indeed, are most myths which tell of divine revolts. Similarly, the tales of Zeus's numerous amorous adventures that are linked with specific

districts in so many parts of Greece, are a euphemistic statement of the old enforced 'marriage' between the conquering god and the local form of the Great Goddess—a union which, in many cases, will actually have taken place between the war-leader of the victorious invaders and the queen or high priestess of the captured district.

Also at about this time the old system of matrilineal succession died out and its place was taken by the custom of the invaders—a son now succeeded his father and no longer, as under the old order, left his father's home to marry into the family of his bride. Instead it was she who left her father's house and went to live in the house of her husband's father; while it was her brother who inherited the lands and rights which would, in earlier days, have been hers and her husband's. But in many myths the old order lives on. To mention but one of these; Menelaus leaves Argolis to go to Sparta where he marries Helen, the (supposed) daughter of the King, and in due time becomes himself the ruler of Sparta by virtue of his marriage. Small wonder then, one might think, that he so readily forgave Helen's adultery! An example of later custom is seen in the marriage of one of Helen's unsuccessful suitors, Odysseus. Rejected by Helen he woos Penelope, the daughter of a Spartan chieftain and in spite of her father's objections, persuades her to leave Sparta and go with him to his own home on the island of Ithaca.

Gradually, over the centuries there evolved a similar pattern of worship for all Greece, and a pantheon of deities was established, though inevitably divergencies and inconsistencies remained for all the efforts of the ancient poets and mythographers who sought to explain and reconcile them.

Foremost in this Greek pantheon in historical times were the so-called Twelve Olympians—the elite amongst the gods and goddesses. They were believed to dwell with Zeus, their lord—and for some of them, their father—in palaces surrounding his stronghold on Mount Olympus, though they did not always live in amity with him. Now and then one or another of them, including Hera, his queen, would rebel against his authority. This situation was a reflection of the conditions prevailing in earlier times since in just the same manner did the chieftains of a king sometimes challenge his authority; and the lesser kings of Greece flout the leadership of the high King Agamemnon in Homer's *Iliad*.

The list of the Twelve Olympians was modified from time to time, but they are most frequently given as Zeus, Poseidon, Hera, Demeter, Apollo, Artemis, Aphrodite, Ares, Hephaestus, Hermes, Athene and Hestia. Latterly Hestia was usually replaced by the important newcomer from Thrace, Dionysus.

In spite of that deposition, however, Hestia was highly revered by all as a very ancient and important aspect of the Great Goddess. The hearth where she was believed to preside was the very heart of the home, and was moreover, like the altar of a medieval church, a safe asylum where a suppliant might beg the protection of the householder. Sacred oaths were sworn by her name and since she was not only the fire of the hearth, but also the sacred fire of the temple altar, the first portion of every sacrifice was offered to Hestia. In most towns she had her public sanctuary with its own hearth fire from which emigrant Greeks, setting off to found a colony, would carry embers to kindle the sacred fire in their new home.

Just as Greek mythology has been affected and modified by cults from other lands, so the most important of the Greek gods exerted a strong influence on both the gods of the Roman pantheon and the earlier, native Etruscan deities. The chief Roman gods in their latest forms are usually equated with the Twelve Olympians. In western Europe from the time of the Renaissance, when there was an immense revival of interest in classical art and learning, until comparatively recently the deities of Greece have been referred to by the names of their Roman counterparts (except by Greek scholars). And even today, though we may differentiate between the two groups of deities and call the gods of Greece by their own Greek names, we still latinize the spelling. For the convenience of any reader to whom the Roman gods are more familiar than those of Greece, the principal deities (and one famous hero) of both mythologies are listed here, each one named being paired with his or her counterpart.

Greek	*Roman*
Zeus	Jupiter
Poseidon	Neptune
Hades	Pluto
Hera	Juno
Demeter	Ceres
Persephone	Proserpina
Hestia	Vesta
Apollo	Apollo
Artemis	Diana
Aphrodite	Venus
Eros	Cupid
Ares	Mars
Hephaestos	Vulcan
Hermes	Mercury
Dionysus	Bacchus
Asklepios	Aesculapius
Heracles	Hercules

There were sceptics and atheists amongst the intellectuals, but to the average Greek of the classical period, as to his ancestors, the gods were present everywhere, though unseen. In

appearance they were thought of as being like men, only far more beautiful and with infinitely nobler minds, and that is how they were depicted in art—idealized and perfect. As well as being more beautiful the gods were immeasurably more skilled than their worshippers. Indeed, over whatsoever craft or skill—artistic, domestic, military or any other—a deity presided, he was unquestionably the greatest of all the practitioners of that craft or skill. If a man possessed any talent or rejoiced in any measure of skill it was reckoned as a gift from the gods and therefore the Greeks believed it fitting that he should not waste it, but use it to the best of his ability, so that he might, in a modest way, resemble the gods themselves. However, it was imperative that it should only be in a modest way, since to think oneself too like a god was to offend against the gods and to be guilty of *hubris*—reckless pride. Once again that favourite Greek maxim admonishes: 'Nothing to excess'.

Just as their beauty and their skills were far beyond any to which a man might attain, so the gods were also above the restrictions which governed human behaviour and were not expected to follow the rules of conduct which had been laid down for man. This attitude to divine morality prevailed largely unchanged throughout the whole age during which the Greek gods were worshipped. Even at the latest period, when high standards of human morality had long replaced the early unenlightened ways, the gods were still not expected to conform; and in the popular conception only two gods developed to show any ethical improvement in attributes and characteristics. These two were Zeus and Apollo, the two deities who had the strongest influence on every sphere and aspect of Greek life and thought. Because they believed their gods to be everywhere and in everything, and because they were bound by no inflexible dogmas or doctrines, the Greeks found no difficulty in reconciling science and religion. All scientific discoveries were merely attributed to the Gods' powers.

Though the Greeks felt reverence for their gods, they could laugh at them as well and see no sin in it. As early as Homer they were laughing—the Homeric *Hymn to Hermes* contains humourous anecdotes of some of Hermes' merry pranks—and in the *Iliad*, Homer makes several of the gods and goddesses look very foolish indeed on the battlefield, when they interfere in the conduct of the war. In later literature there are frequent divine appearances in drama. Often the god enters only towards the end of the action— as the original *deus ex machina*, in fact—and resolves the difficulties of the protagonists and closes the drama on a suitably uplifting note. But sometimes he plays a longer and more important role— and a role, moreover, which is not always dignified. It is hard to recognize the beautiful and rather terrifying young Dionysus of the *Bacchae* of Euripides when we meet him again as a figure of fun in the *Frogs* of the comic poet Aristophanes—who was no liberal-minded 'modern' like Euripides, but an unashamed reactionary who hankered after the good old days. If we worshipped Dionysus, the divine protector of theatres and the deity who presided over dramatic art, we would hardly dare to show him as an absurd, cowardly dilettante, with less dignity than his own slave. Yet it is all very entertaining and laughable, and the Greeks saw no blasphemy in it.

In their towns and cities the Greeks worshipped their gods in the beautiful temples which they built to honour them —most often on some ancient hallowed site. Though any individual might approach any of the gods on his own behalf, by archaic and classical times worship was principally communal and public. The most elaborate rites and ceremonies were those observed by the state on behalf of all the people; but each small township, as well as every local clan or family of importance, also had its own particular observances.

Human sacrifice was abandoned in Greece as unworthy and degrading from about the sixth century BC, though animals continued to be offered to the gods, as well as fruits and flowers. An integral part of the public religious ceremonies was a solemn procession through the streets of the city to the temple of victims and objects sacred to the deity concerned. There, with hymns and prayers—often written by the most famed and respected poets and musicians of the day—the victims would be sacrificed in an elaborate and orderly ritual, and the ceremony would end with the worshippers partaking of a feast of the flesh of the sacrificed animals.

These public, civic cults were fixed according to a state calendar and though many of them were connected with the vital affairs of agriculture, through the years they had come to be celebrated on days which did not always correspond with the real seasons of the farming year. This was not so much the case in country districts where, then as now, work was ruled by weather conditions and the harvest was celebrated at the time of its gathering.

From around the end of the fifth century BC the cult of a latecomer to the Greek pantheon—Asklepios, the god of medicine—grew in popularity. The swift advance of his worship coincided with a development in philosophical ideas about the importance of the individual; and even those thinkers who were inclined to feel sceptical towards the Olympian deities paid respect to the gentle healer and acknowledged the worth of his cult. By Christian times his worship was widespread and strong and of all the gods of the Greeks, Asklepios was the only one whose cult presented any danger to the march of Christianity. As paganism was crushed out, yet still the loyal worshippers of Asklepios resisted, while many of his shrines were appropriated and given to wonder-working Christian saints. And thus, not quite everything that was good in the religion of the Greeks was lost and destroyed by the intolerance of monotheism; a little—albeit a very little— was for a time preserved to bring comfort to men.

Barbara Leonie Picard

I
BEFORE THE OLYMPIANS

1

Plate 1

The southern gateway of the palace of Knossos, with the horns of consecration.
The Minoan culture of Crete saw the Aegean civilization at its highest point:
the many currents had mingled for thousands of years before this remarkable
flowering. The archaeologists have shown how much the concept of the
Earth Goddess—the Mother—dominated the religious practices of the Greek
people in ancient times; the serpent and bull symbols which recur so frequently
in connection with her in Knossos are both expressions of fertility and man
came to realize very early that without her goodwill he might have no harvest, no
fruitfulness. She was still propitiated even when alien gods seemed to have
usurped her place.

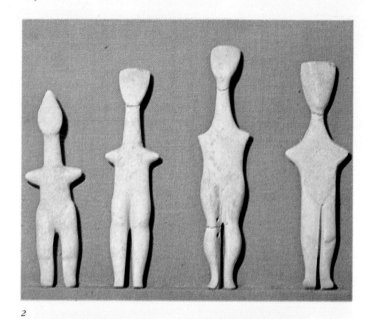

2

Plate 2

A group of marble figures from the island of
Naxos. They date from about 2,500 BC and
are typical of the many pieces commonly called
Cycladic, from the group of islands of which
Naxos is one. Their great antiquity combines with
a lack of evidence to invest them with mystery—it is
impossible to determine exactly what they were.
Loosely referred to as idols or fertility figures, their
chief interest lies in the fact that legend connects the
Cyclades with Crete: the islands were said to have
been ruled by the Carians, who were driven out
by Minos, King of Crete. The Carians were
from Asia Minor, and the features common to all
religions of the eastern Mediterranean were to some
extent due to the exchange of ideas.

3   4.

Plate 3

A primitive vase found in a tomb at Koumasi in
Crete. It is probably from the same period as the
Cycladic figures but here an attempt has been made
to express a positive idea. The serpent was an
ancient symbol of fertility and renewal and therefore
an apt symbol for the Mother. It was also a sexual
symbol, being at once phallic and a swallower.
In this crude representation a snake is draped over
the shoulders of a female figure.

Plate 4

Here is the same idea, but presented by the
sophisticated Cretans at the height of the Minoan
culture, between the eighteenth and fifteenth
centuries BC. This beautiful terracotta figurine is
thought by some to represent a serpent goddess
but it is more likely to be the figure of a priestess.
That she serves the Mother is seen by the snakes
twined round her arms, while the conical
headdress suggests that she is dressed for a ceremony.
The rest of her costume was common to the
ladies of the court of Knossos; they are all seen, in
both statuettes and wall paintings, to be wearing
gowns which lie open at the top to give full
exposure to the breasts; the gowns are all tightly
waisted and fall in flounces to the ankles.

5

Plate 5

The bull-leaping fresco from the palace of Knossos.
The sport looks dangerous—seizing the horns and
somersaulting over the bull's back would
require remarkable timing and a high degree
of fitness. But games in Crete (if this was indeed
a game) probably occurred at festivals, as they did
in Greece, and the bull symbol is ubiquitous in
the art of the Cretans. Like the serpent it was an
important cult animal; it also expressed fertility but
added the quality of strength. The story of
Theseus and the Minotaur—the offspring of a queen
who mated with a bull—took place in Crete.

Plate 6

A ritual vase in the shape of a bull's head carved
from black steatite and inlaid with rock crystal
and shell. It is a fine example of the Minoan art of
the fifteenth century BC. With a mother goddess
in the supreme position it was inevitable that
her consort should be expressed as the embodiment
of male strength and creative energy. It was
probably from this association that the myth of
Theseus and the Minotaur grew; the later
Greeks did not give the myths their form until many
centuries had passed, and they connected Crete and
the figure of Theseus with a heroic age. The
gods they honoured were rather human and like
themselves—not the expression of natural
forces imperfectly understood and therefore to be
feared and respected. Theseus, one of their great
ancestors, would not have been honoured if he had
crossed the seas to fight a mere man; the bull
motif would have provided the Greeks'
imagination with a monster, and their hero with a
worthy adversary.

7

Plate 7

The bull as a sacrifice. From the Minoan site at Hagia Triada comes this sarcophagus, carved from a block of limestone and covered with white plaster on which scenes from the funeral rites were painted. This one shows the sacrifice of a bull which was bound and laid on the altar; a priestess stands on the left and a musician plays in the background. The blood will drain into the vessel at the foot of the altar. The coffin dates from about the fifteenth century BC.

8   9

Plate 8 and 9

There is ample evidence that mainland Greece was familiar with the customs and beliefs of Crete—indeed at this time in history it is likely that they were widespread in the Aegean. This gold cup was found in a royal tomb at Vaphio, south of Sparta. It is Cretan work and shows the capture of bulls, probably wild ones. They might be for use in the arena for the bull-leaping game, or for sacrifice, or simply for breeding. Above a bull has been netted and thrown. Left it is being hobbled by a hunter who wears the long hair and tightly-waisted kilt familiar from the frescoes at Knossos. The cup dates from the sixteenth century BC, when the Mycenean culture was beginning to grow in strength. Later it would completely overcome the Minoan.

II
THE COMING OF ORDER

10

Plate 10

Little is known for certain about the gods of the Greeks in the dark centuries that followed the destruction of the Minoan culture. The Indo-European migrations were bringing new men down into the peninsula in the early part of the second millennium and a new, male-orientated society was mingling with the old. The Achaeans—those described by Homer—came in the thirteenth century BC; they were warlike and ruthless and the tide seemed to be irreversible. A god-king challenged the Mother. Tradition, however, dies hard, and the new All-powerful was given a childhood in Crete. The picture shows the cave of Dicte, on the Aegean Hill, where Rhea, the mother of Zeus, hid her son from his father Cronus.

11

12

13

Plate 11

The shaft graves at Mycenae. Towards the end of the second millennium the Achaeans were followed by the Dorians; a usurper race was in fact displaced by one even more powerful though adhering to much the same religious ideas. Sky-gods replaced the Mother in all parts of Greece, a process often brought about by the taking of wives from the old ruling clans, and imposing a new religion together with a new order. But it was by no means a peaceful process; and the troubled world to which the Homeric heroes returned after the fall of Troy is probably a reflection of this.

Plate 12

The castration of Uranus. The stories of the gods and their beginnings were given a definite shape by Homer and Hesiod, and were generally accepted by the eighth and seventh centuries BC. Ge, or Mother Earth, emerged from Chaos and bore Uranus, the starry universe, who became her consort. All their children were hated by Uranus who feared any challenge to his rule, and the Titans, the Giants, the Cyclops and Cronus were confined to the nether world. The angry Earth Mother released her youngest son, Cronus, and encouraged him to castrate his father and rule in his place.

Plate 13

The peak of Mount Olympus. When Cronus succeeded to his father's place he took his sister Rhea as his consort. (Interestingly, Rhea was probably the name by which the Mother was known in Crete.) Warned by Ge that one of his children would destroy him, he followed his father and swallowed his children as soon as they were born. The enraged Rhea gave him a stone to swallow in place of his third son, Zeus, whom she hid until he reached manhood. Zeus then enlisted the help of Cyclops, Giants, some of the Titans (including Prometheus) and waged war on Cronus and the rest of the Titans from Mount Olympus. Zeus was victorious; Cronus disappeared from myth and the stage was set for the ordering of the gods and their place in the consciousness of the Greeks. Even Zeus was insecure to begin with though he was eventually to rule unchallenged.

Plate 14

The great archaeologist Schliemann undertook the excavation of Mycenae which was the seat of the High King Agamemnon and the gold mask is from one of the royal graves. When Schliemann lifted it he saw for a brief moment the face of a fair-bearded king, before it crumbled to dust. He sent a telegram to the King of Greece: 'I have gazed upon the face of Agamemnon.' It is certain now that the fair-bearded king will never be identified and there is no way of ascertaining who he was. But the intense drama of that moment in the grave is easy to imagine.

15

Plate 15

One of the challenges that Zeus and the other
Olympians had to face was the rebellion of
the Giants who were born to Ge when the blood of
the castrated Uranus fell on her. A detail from the
frieze of the Syphian treasury at Delphi shows one of
the Giants attacked by a lion—the creature of
Cybele. Cybele was an Asiatic goddess from the
Near East, the Great Mother, and identified by the
Greeks with Rhea. Her cult found its way to
Greece by way of the Greeks of Phrygia, in
Asia Minor.

Plate 16

Prometheus in Greek mythology is not only man's
first friend; in some traditions he is also his
creator, having fashioned him from clay and
breathed life into him. Prometheus learned much
from Athene, at whose birth he assisted, and
he passed his knowledge on to mankind.
His benefactions to man were a source of Zeus'
wrath, which was further aroused by the
knowledge that Prometheus possessed a secret that
could end his supremacy. He ordered that
Prometheus be chained to a rock in the Caucusus,
and every day sent an eagle to feed on his liver,
which was resored each succeeding night; the
torture would thus be perpetual.

17

Plate 17

The secret that only Prometheus knew was that Zeus, who could not control his lusts, would one day seduce the nereid, Thetis. Any son of Thetis would prove to be greater than his father—and Zeus would fall. Eventually the two were reconciled: Prometheus told Zeus the secret, and Zeus granted him the immortality that the centaur, Chiron, was longing to surrender. Chiron was suffering from an incurable wound but being immortal could never die and find release from pain. Prometheus was possibly a fire god in origin; but the struggle with Zeus serves to underline the rejection of the former way of things—there were to be no more challenges to the king of the gods. Prometheus is one of the most interesting figures in Greek mythology, and the central figure in one of the tragedies of Aeschylus who presents him as the personification of man's eternal resistance to arbitrary fate. In this fourth-century Corinthian terracotta Thetis is seen riding a sea-horse, and carrying the helmet of Achilles—whose mother she was to become, though not by Zeus.

18

Plate 18

Zeus and another challenge. He is about to engage in combat with the monster Typhon. The son of Ge, he challenged the sky god, and the sight of him struck terror into the hearts of the other Olympians, who disguised themselves as animals and fled. Zeus got much the worst part of the opening struggle; Typhon severed the sinews of his hands and feet and left him lying helpless in a cave. He was rescued by Hermes and Pan, and his sinews restored. He was eventually victorious, and Zeus buried Typhon under Mount Etna which still heaves and belches smoke with the struggles of the monster within. Painting on a water jar, sixth century BC.

III
THE OLYMPIANS

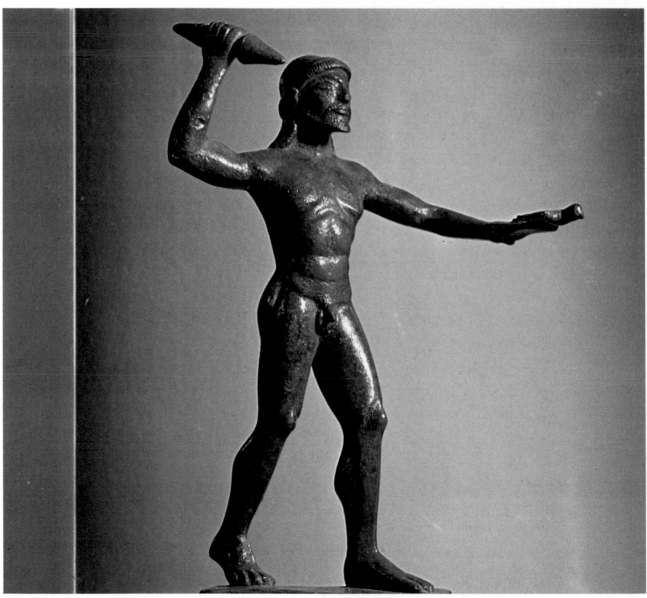

19

Plate 19

A Greek bronze of Zeus bearing a thunderbolt. As the sky god he is the
embodiment of an idea which was ancient long before the Dorians found their
way down into Greece, and can be definitely identified in the religion of
ancient India. He was originally the Indo-European *weather* god as well—he who
controlled the thunder and the rain, a deity of the first importance to migratory
herdsmen. The third son of Cronus according to Hesiod, he is made the first
son by Homer, who also describes the division of the world among the
three sons: Poseidon was given the seas and Hades the underworld; Zeus himself
retained the heavens. He ruled by the counsel of Ge—through all the changes
in Greek religion the Mother remained. She could both foretell the future and act
as the instrument of fate. The bronze is fifth-century and comes from Dodona,
where there was an oracle of Zeus.

20

Plate 20

The most famous temple of Zeus in classical Greece was the one at Olympia—not, as might be supposed, somewhere near Mount Olympus; Olympia was in Elis, in the Peloponnese. The Olympic Games were held there, every fourth year, and in the sacred precinct were two temples, one to Hera and a magnificent one to Zeus. It was 220 feet long and 90 feet wide; the columns were 30 feet high. Next to Delphi Olympia was the greatest religious centre of Greece. It retained its position until the fourth century AD, when the Emperor Theodosius, a Christian, issued an edict enjoining the destruction of all pagan sites.

Plate 21

Zeus enthroned. This impressive marble statue shows him as ruler and father. He was the dispenser of good and evil in the fortunes of men, and the giver of laws that ruled the course of events. He had many titles: defender of the house, defender of the hearth, upholder of the right to liberty, maintainer of the laws of hospitality, guardian of property. He was also *Chthonios*, the god of the earth and the giver of fertility, a title which showed the persistence of the connection in Greek minds of the male god as a consort. Despite the extraordinary virtues which were uttered in his praise Zeus was, paradoxically, a very human god. His rages were accepted as natural bad temper and his casual disregard of marriage laws no obstacle to an acceptance of him as both lawgiver and *paterfamilias*. His love affairs with members of both sexes were the subject of comedy and his treatment of Prometheus seen as a regrettable stage in the establishment of order.

Plate 22

The marriage of Zeus and Hera, from the fifth-century temple at Selinunte. Hera was one of the children of Cronus and Rhea and thus sister as well as wife to Zeus. Her character in Greek mythology is not attractive and her moments of angry spite were almost always caused through jealousy of her husband's amours. Certainly he was wayward enough to test the most patient wife but the many stories of his infidelities can be traced to something more than mere lustfulness. The ascendancy of the god, as opposed to the goddess with whom the native Greeks had been familiar for centuries, was often accomplished by the union of a local deity with the newcomer —and the object of his lust can often be identified in this way. Since many royal houses claimed descent from him his extra-marital adventures were also required to cover a very wide field.

22

Plate 23

One of the loves of Zeus was Europa, the daughter of Agenor, King of Tyre. She used to walk with her companions near the seashore, and one day she noticed a beautiful white bull among her father's cattle. She hung garlands on his horns and then climbed on his back—whereupon the bull plunged into the sea and swam away with her. He carried her to the island of Crete and took his pleasure of her there, and the children of this union were Minos, Rhadamanthus and Sarpedon. The reigning king of Crete, Asterius, married Europa and having no sons of his own adopted hers. The connections with Crete in the myth is interesting as it raises the factor of the bull cult. Europa is seen here on a sixth-century vase painting from Caere.

23

24

Plate 24

Zeus in the guise of a swan pays court to Leda—an affair which was to have serious consequences. She was the daughter of Thestios, King of Aetolia and the wife of Tyndareus, King of Sparta. Leda liked to bathe in the river Eurotas, where one day she saw a swan swimming beside her. The swan being Zeus, the sequel was inevitable— though Leda must have been rather disconcerted to find herself laying eggs as the result of her dalliance. However, Tyndareus lay with her that night too and there is no record in the myths that he found his wife's way of bearing children unusual. Three children emerged from the egg: Castor and Pollux, and the beautiful Helen.

25

26

Plate 25

The story of Leda and the swan may have arisen from a memory of a nature cult; they were familiar in Greece and Crete in early times. This gold pendant is from Aegina but the workmanship is Cretan. A god or a priest is standing on a lotus plant, holding a swan in each hand. *c* 2,000 BC.

Plate 26

Hera was the legitimate consort of Zeus and occupied first place among the goddesses of the Greeks. Homer describes her as 'Argive' Hera, a reference to the origin of her cult in Argos. Her character was formidable and there is good reason to see her as the survival of a powerful cult of the Mother in Argos—marrying her was perhaps the only way open to Zeus of reconciling his power with hers: that is to say that the new Greeks found this way of reconciling the original people with themselves; Hera, as Mother, would have had no consort at all or else one of little importance. The patron and guardian of marriage, Hera also watched over women in childbirth and her blessing was sought to bring fruitfulness to the womb. She makes a striking appearance in the myth of the Argonauts as the befriender of Jason against his enemy Pelias; Pelias had withheld his homage to the goddess—a dangerous thing to do where Hera was concerned. In this Attic red-figured vase she is seen with Hebe, her daughter by Zeus who was cup-bearer to the gods.

Plate 27

Hera's temple at Agrigento, the ancient Acragas. Acragas was on the south-west coast of Sicily, an island popular with emigrant Greeks throughout their history. The city prospered through its trade with Carthage and built superb temples in the classical style; the poet Pindar in particular was lavish in his praise. The city, which was founded in the sixth century BC, was sacked by the Carthaginians during one of their conflicts with Rome in 405.

28

Plate 28

Hera gives the charge of the winds to Aeolus. Zeus himself found the winds a troublesome responsibility; they might, when his attention was diverted, have blown both earth and sea away. He confined them within a cliff that floated in the Tyrrhenian Sea among some islands, and to those islands Aeolus sailed in search of a home. That the bestowal of the winds on Aeolus should have been the action of Hera is explained by one authority in terms of Hera's original character as the Mother: the winds were her messengers. Delacroix's painting is distinctly Romantic in tone but the figure of Aeolus, after whom the Aeolian islands were named, has the appropriate heroic look.

29

Plate 29

Poseidon, the brother of Zeus and the lord of the seas. He was also, and probably more significantly, the god chiefly connected with horses, which suggests that his origin was very ancient indeed and dated from the time of the migrations. (The importance of the sea to the Greeks came much later.) The horse was a creature of enormous importance to the Indo-European migrants; it provided transport, food, clothing and was a visible symbol of fertility. Poseidon's title, *Hippios*, identifies him firmly and the horse appears again and again in the traditions of the Greeks. When Greek religion was formalized the ancient deity was probably given the domain that seemed closest to his original character, following the ancient idea that river (water) gods were horses and the symbolism of the white crests of the waves. Poseidon was not, apparently, content with his portion; he squabbled with Athene for the possession of Attica and with Hera for that of Aegina.

Plate 30

Amarble group from Smyrna, dating from the second century AD. The sculpture is notable not only for its late date but also because it actually shows Poseidon and Demeter together. The myth concerning them is very strange and probably a confusion of several different stories. Poseidon lusted after Demeter (his sister according to Hesiod) but she would have none of him, grieving as she was over her lost daughter Persephone. To escape his attentions Demeter turned herself into a mare, and slipped in among the horse herds of Arcadia. However her transformation had not escaped the keen eye of Poseidon; he promptly turned himself into a stallion and joined the herd too. The furious Demeter soon found herself mounted by a triumphant Poseidon. The offspring of this remarkable coupling was the magical horse, Arion, who became the property of Adrastus, King of Argos.

30

Plate 31

Poseidon's temple on the promontory at Sounion, the cape which forms the southern tip of Attica. The cape was a welcome landmark for the Athenian sailors making for the Piraeus and there was a temple to Poseidon under construction which was destroyed by the Persians before it could be completed. The columns which survive are from the marble temple to the god of the seas built by the Athenians in the late fifth century BC. It was at Cape Sounion that Apollo struck down Menelaus' pilot on the voyage back from Sparta. Menelaus was delayed and his brother Agamemnon, returning alone to Mycenae, fell victim to Clytemnestra and Aegisthus.

31

Plate 32

Demeter, the goddess who more than any other personified for the Greeks the timeless idea of the fruitful earth. She was an ancient deity of mainland Greece, the corn-goddess on whom survival depended. In later times she is also the sorrowing mother of Persephone who was abducted by Hades, the god of the underworld. Her anguished search for her daughter led her to neglect the earth and it ceased to be fruitful: Zeus had to intervene lest the earth became completely barren and mankind perished. She was at Eleusis when her daughter was restored to her, and the Mysteries of her cult were celebrated there: those and the great festival of the Thesmophoria (of Demeter Thesmophoros— the bringer of treasures) were the most popular and widely attended of all Greek religion. Demeter as the sorrowing mother is strikingly portrayed in this marble of the fourth century BC.

32

33

34

35

Plate 33

Demeter and Kore. This vase painting shows mother and daughter (*kore*—maiden) with ears of corn. 'The maiden' was another way of referring to Persephone and this lends weight to the opinion that she was simply another aspect of the same goddess. The ancient Mother was in some respects the eternal woman—the mother who bore the maiden, who became a mother, who later attended on other births, who laid out the dead, who died herself, who was renewed as the maiden, who became a mother. . . . The myth relates how Persephone, at the intervention of Zeus, would have been permanently returned by Hades; but she had eaten the food of the dead— four pomegranate seeds—and was really bound to Hades for ever. In the end the god of the underworld exacted a price for her release: for each of the seeds she ate she would have to spend a month with him. This was agreed: each year Persephone returns to Hades, and winter falls upon the land.

Plate 34

Hades, seen with Persephone on a Greek amphora found in Apulia. He was the brother of Zeus, Poseidon, and Demeter also; Hesiod's arrangement of the family of the Olympians makes him a lustful uncle. To the Greeks he was the ruler of the world of the dead and they also gave this name to his realm, which was separated from the world of the living by the river Styx. The dead were ferried across by Charon, whose fee for the service was placed in the mouth of the corpse. The burial rites were therefore all-important. At the entrance to Hades stood the watch-dog Cerberus, who prevented those who entered from ever leaving again. Hades helped in the defeat of Cronus by stealing his weapons, and while not regarded with affection by the Greeks he exacted a great deal of respect. But he was not a *punisher*—the Greeks had no conception of any god who might be equated with Satan.

Plate 35

The association of Persephone and Hades is probably a strand of the ancient veneration of the Mother as the bestower of all things and she to whom all departed when life had run its course. Not surprisingly this aspect of the Mother was rarely expressed but the Maiden and Mother partners were often to be seen in votive figures and works of art. This sixth-century terracotta shows them as identical. It comes from Corinth and is now in the British Museum.

Plate 36

Triptolemos was the son of the King of Eleusis who offered kindness to the exhausted Demeter after her wanderings. He alone recognized the goddess and it was he who told her that her daughter was in the possession of Hades. When Demeter was reunited with Persephone she rewarded Triptolemos with the knowledge of agriculture, and through him initiated the Mysteries at Eleusis. He was thereafter regarded as a culture hero; the spread of agriculture as the basis for an ordered and increasingly civilized life was attributed to him, and he was honoured at the Mysteries and at the Thesmophoria. He is seen here as a boy, receiving from Demeter the first sprig of corn. Bas-relief of the fifth century BC, now in the National Museum, Athens.

36

Plate 37

The ruins of the fifth-century temple of Demeter at Paestum. Paestum, which lies on the coast below Naples, was founded by Greek colonists in 600 BC. It flourished for centuries and was a wealthy city, as the impressive ruins testify; but the encroaching marshes made it unhealthy and it was gradually deserted during the Roman Empire.

37

39

Plate 38

The Acropolis, seen from the Philopappus Hill. The word means 'upper city' and an eminence was commonly chosen in ancient times to give the city itself a citadel. The flat rock is 200 feet higher than Athens and, fittingly, it was the setting for the most famous temple ever built—the Parthenon, the temple of Athene Parthenos or Athene the Maiden. She was the patron goddess of Athens; the myth tells of the rivalry for the possession of Attica, and how Poseidon disputed Athene's claim. A council of the gods declared that the victor should be the one who gave to man the greatest gift. Poseidon struck the ground with his trident, and created the first horse. But Athene planted an olive tree and she was adjudged the victor. The meaning of the myth is plain: it is generally agreed by scholars that the figure of Athene goes back to archaic times, long before the Greeks arrived in the peninsula.

Plate 39

Athene was the daughter of Zeus and Metis—an unwilling Metis who did her best to escape the god's attentions. Ge (Mother Earth) warned Zeus that the child of this union would be a girl but if he persisted in his attentions and she conceived a second child it would be a son, and depose him just as he had deposed his father Cronus. Zeus took no chances with any child of Metis: as soon as he could get close enough to her he swallowed her whole. In due course he began to feel violent headaches, which increased in severity so that his howling began to shake the heavens. Hermes divined the cause of discomfort; he fetched Hephaestos, who split Zeus' skull open. Athene sprang forth with a great shout, fully armed.

Plate 40

The Parthenon, constructed during the age of
Pericles between 447 and 438 BC. It was built
entirely of Pentelic marble and its perfect
proportions combine strength and grace; it is
the Doric style at the peak of perfection. The lovely
temple to Athene was revered for nearly a
thousand years; then the Byzantines gutted the
interior to make it a Christian church. This
barbarism was furthered by the Franks in
the thirteenth century AD, by the Turks in the
fifteenth, and by the Venetians in the seventeenth
century, so the Parthenon was a ruin when
Lord Elgin removed the sculptures in the nineteenth.
Many of them are in the British Museum.

Plate 41

Apollo, as the Etruscans saw him. A terracotta
statue of the fifth century BC from Veii depicts
a rather sinister god. Apollo was the son of
Zeus and Leto, daughter of the Titans
Coeus and Phoebe. Leto was the victim of
Hera's jealousy, and for fear of the goddess's
wrath no land would receive Leto when her time
drew near. She made her way to Ortygia near Delos;
the two islands floated in the sea, and only became
anchored after Leto's children were delivered. First
she gave birth to a girl, Artemis, who was no
sooner born than she helped her mother
cross to Delos. Apollo was born there on the
north side of Mount Cynthus and was a favoured
child from the beginning: Themis fed him on nectar
and ambrosia, and Hephaestos brought him arms
when he was only four days old. Apollo was a
late-comer among the gods of Greece, and probably
had his origins among the migrating peoples.
But the conception of a golden son, just and
beautiful and a benefactor, is a popular one and his
counterpart can be found in many mythologies.

42

43

Plate 42

Mount Parnassus in the spring, still crowned by the winter snows. When he left Delos Apollo went in search of the serpent Python, who had at Hera's orders tormented Leto in her wanderings. He found him on Parnassus and wounded him with arrows; but Python managed to escape and fled to the oracle of Mother Earth at Delphi. Apollo dared to follow him into the sacred place where he killed him by the chasm from where the oracular utterances came.

Plate 43

Delphi lies on the south-west spur of Mount Parnassus and was an oracular shrine in the time before the Olympians, and the Greeks wisely chose to maintain its reputation. When Apollo killed Python there he was required to undergo purification for defilining a holy place; but he coaxed the art of prophecy from the god Pan (significantly, Pan was a nature god as old as the Mother herself) and then returned to Delphi. He seized the shrine for himself and Delphi became the most venerated site in Greece, the object of endless pilgrimages where the priests of Apollo sat on a tripod over the sacred chasm giving the answers to the questions of suppliants. The Delphic Oracle was the supreme authority on matters of religion. Only two other gods were represented at Delphi, Dionysus and Athene. The picture shows the Tholos, one of the buildings in the precinct dedicated to Athene. It dates from the fourth century BC.

Plate 44

Apollo with his lyre, pouring a libation. He was the god of light (Phoebus, the bright), youth, prophecy and music—especially of the lyre. His other charge, the care of flocks and herds, points to his origin among the Indo-European migrants. Apollo's companions as the god of music—and of most the arts—were Dionysus as the patron of the theatre, and the Muses, the daughters of Zeus by Mnemosyne (memory). Apollo was a dangerous god to be involved with— King Midas was given asses' ears and Marsyas the satyr was flayed alive when they both doubted Apollo's musical supremacy—and it thus seems strange that the Greeks seemed to associate him with moral excellence. His cult in Delphi had an enormous influence in the extension of tolerance; it prescribed expiation for all crimes and actively discouraged the ancient idea of vengeance. But the Delphic Apollo is the later personification; the ancient god may well have been one to fear. The illustration is from a Greek dish of the fifth century BC, now in the museum at Delphi.

44

Plate 45

A relief of the first century BC showing a Muse playing a lyre. When the gods defeated the Titans Zeus was asked to create divinities capable of celebrating the victory. He lay with Mnmosyne for nine nights and the nine daughters of this union were the Muses. Though their preferred home was Mount Helicon they liked to visit Parnassus where they sought the waters of the Castalian spring and where they enjoyed the company of Apollo. The waters of the spring were used in purification rites in the temple at Delphi and were also given to the Pythoness (priestess) of the oracle to drink.

45

46

47

Plate 46

An early Greek terracotta, probably a votive
offering, which represents the goddess
Artemis. Homer describes Artemis as Mistress
of Beasts and the description was as true of the
goddess the Greeks venerated as it was of the Mother
of whom she is another aspect. Like her twin
brother Apollo she bore a name which was
not Greek in origin but unlike him she was an
original deity of Greece and the Aegean. Her origins,
like those of so many Greek gods, clung to her
even when she was transformed into an Olympian;
thus she is a virgin goddess while at the same
time a giver of fertility, and her domain is the wild
earth, the forests and hills where she hunts. Again,
her pleading with Asklepios to restore life to the
dead Hippolytus suggests a very human and
womanly love. In the tragedy by Euripides
Hippolytus was presented as a man of perfect
purity—a fit companion for Artemis. Possibly their
story is a survival of the goddess's original
character; as an aspect of the Mother she would
have had a consort. The terracotta shown
here portrays the Mistress of Beasts carrying
a small unidentifiable animal, possibly a fawn.
Small animals were sacrificed to her at her annual
festival at Patrae.

Plate 47

Much more in keeping with the character of the
Mother from whom she stemmed is the Artemis
of Ephesus, the Ionian city which in classical
times was a great seaport and the rival of
Antioch and Alexandria. The cult of Artemis
the giver of fertility had an ancient centre near the
city and it was there that King Croesus ordered the
building of a temple to her, a building which was
to become one of the wonders of the ancient
world. It was from Ephesus, not from Greece, that
the cult of the goddess found its way to Rome.
There, as Diana, she exacted the same confusion of
venerations that she enjoyed in Greece. The city
of Ephesus eventually declined; the silt of the
Cayster river choked the harbour and now
the remains of her glory lie several miles inland.

Plate 48

The virgin huntress. In this manifestation Artemis
appears in the *Iliad*—and cuts rather a poor
figure. She tries conclusions with the other
Olympians present at the siege of Troy (the gods
took definite sides in the struggle) and arouses the
wrath of Hera, who tells her scornfully that the
killing of animals is her proper place. However, if
she *will* challenge her betters she must suffer
the consequences: Hera then seizes Artemis' wrists in
one hand and grabs her quiver and arrows with
the other; she beats her victim about the
head with them until the hapless Artemis breaks
free and flies weeping to Olympus to be comforted
by her father Zeus. Nevertheless Artemis was a
firm favourite with women, especially those in the
humbler walks of life who probably knew her
best in her original form.

49

Plate 49

Hephaestos, the divine artificer and god of fire was the maker of magical things for gods and men, such as the armour of Achilles and Agamemnon's sceptre. The son of Zeus and Hera, he was such a sickly child at birth that Hera in disgust flung him from Olympus. He fell into the sea where Thetis (the mother of Achilles) and Eurynome found and cared for him, giving him a forge to work in. He made such exquisite jewellery that it attracted the attention of his cold-hearted mother and she had her son brought back to Olympus to take his proper place. Later he intervened in a quarrel between Hera and Zeus who hurled him from Olympus again. He returned to Olympus permanently lamed, but the strength of Hephaestos was in his mighty arms and shoulders which most metal workers develop. His cult centres were always to be found in the cities, where the craft was most intensely practised.

Plate 50

Boucher's painting *The Forges of Vulcan* is based on later accretions; the god is in fact Hephaestos and he is shown here with Aphrodite. The painting suggests domestic harmony; but the marriage was ordered by Zeus and Aphrodite resented being married off to the lame, ungainly smith god. Her lover was Ares, the war god, and the furious Hephaestos constructed an invisible net of bronze to cover the bed, and trapped the guilty pair by pretending to be absent. He then had his revenge when the rest of the Olympians gathered round to laugh at Ares and Aphrodite in their public humiliation.

50

51

Plate 51

The temple of Hephaestos in Athens, north-west of
the Acropolis. Traditionally called the Theseum,
this well-preserved small temple was mis-named,
probably because some of the sculptures relate
to the adventures of Theseus. It is now
generally agreed that it was in fact a shrine to
Hephaestos.

52

Plate 52

Aphrodite, the goddess of love. Homer and Hesiod
differed in their account of her origins; Hesiod said
that she arose from the sea foam which gathered
around the genitals of Uranus when Cronus
cast them down; Homer makes her the
daughter of Zeus and Dione, and therefore
a respectable member of the Olympian pantheon.
She was in fact an ancient goddess of the
eastern Mediterranean and can be equated with
the Asian goddess Astarte. This marble statue from
the Rhodes Museum shows her shaking out her hair
after emerging from the waves. She was worshipped
in Greece in two different manifestations,
Aphrodite Urania (the higher, purer love) and
Aphrodite Pandemos (sensual lust). Her worship
was generally austere but it is interesting to note
that prostitutes regarded her as their patron,
and that there was a sacred prostitution in
her cult at Corinth.

Plate 53

Dionysus returns to Greece to claim his place
among the gods. To the north of Greece, in Thrace
and Macedonia, there was in ancient times a
powerful cult of the spirit of nature and
fertility that expressed itself in orgiastic
rites, human sacrifice and animal worship. This
found its way to Greece around 1,000 BC and its
ecstatic character made an irresistible appeal. At the
centre of the cult was Dionysus, who came to
represent the forces of life and nature in
animals and the fruits of the growing plants;
eventually he was regarded as the god of wine. But
in earlier times there was no need for his followers—
mostly women—to drink; their frenzies were self
induced, and so uncontrollable that it was
dangerous to encounter a band of women in a
Dionysiac frenzy. Animals, and sometimes children,
were torn to pieces and eaten—the belief existing
that to devour a part of an animal was to
partake of the god himself, a true sacramental meal.

53

54

55

Plate 54

An Etruscan terracotta showing the head of a satyr. The spirits of wild life, satyrs were bestial in both their desires and their behaviour and were often pictured with animal characteristics—those of a horse or a goat—to emphasize their connection with fertility. They were attendants on Dionysus, and some myths describe them as taking part in the tutoring of the young god.

Plate 55

An Etruscan bronze of the fifth century BC showing a satyr and a maenad. The maenads were votaries of Dionysus—the word means 'mad women', a description of their behaviour during their frenzied worship. In the play by Euripides, *The Bacchae*, the cult of Dionysus is resisted by Pentheus, King of Thebes, and his mother Agave. Dionysus rouses the women of Thebes to a frenzy and sends them to take part in his rites on the mountainside; then the god reappears in the guise of a votary and persuades the king to spy on them, inducing the same frenzy in Agave that affects the other women. The hapless Pentheus is torn to pieces by the maenads, and Agave returns to the palace carrying a head she has torn from a man's shoulders. Only when her frenzy abates does she realize that the head is her son's. Followers of the god were also called *bakchoi*, and the name Bacchus was the Latin one used by the Romans for their version of Dionysus.

Plate 56

The theatre at Delphi. Dionysus was made respectable by Hesiod, and joined the Olympians as the son of Zeus and Semele. Apollo is credited with the 'taming' of the wilder excesses of Dionysiac religion. During the older, more bestial orgies the maenads often wore masks, and the god was represented by a mask on a pole; the pole was draped with an animal skin but the mask was always human, and this aspect of the cult was the beginning of drama as an art. Apollo admitted Dionysus to his side at Delphi—in other words the powerful cult was admitted to the gentler forms of state religion. By the fifth century BC dramatic festivals were an integral part of Greek culture; one of the most noteworthy festivals was the great Dionysia—the spring festival of Dionysus.

57

Plate 57

Hermes with the infant Dionysus. Hermes was given his place on Olympus by Homer, who made him the son of Zeus and Maia, the daughter of Atlas. In fact he was one of the oldest of the original Greek gods; he was the god of luck and wealth and dreams; patron of merchants—and of thieves; god of the roads and, in Arcadia, of fertility. These ancient attributes were easily metamorphosed when he took his place on Olympus and his most frequent appearance is as a messenger or guide. Here he is seen taking the infant Dionysus to Nysa to entrust him to the care of the nymphs. This famous statue was found in the ruins of the temple of Hera at Olympia and was at first believed to be an original of Praxiteles, *c* 330 BC. It is now generally agreed that the statue is a later copy.

Plate 58

Three Olympians on a Greek amphora. To the left is Hermes wearing his winged sandals, and Dionysus is on the right, crowned with vine leaves and negligently spilling wine from a vessel in his right hand. The goddess in the centre is the virgin of the hearth, Hestia described by Hesiod as the daughter of Cronus and Rhea and thus the sister of Zeus. The hearth fire was the most important thing in the life of early settled man; without it he had no protection or warmth. Obviously it was a sacred principle and the goddess who personified it remained little more than that —there are no myths surrounding her after her establishment on Olympus. She took part in no wars or disputes, and was generally regarded as the most gentle of the family of gods.

IV
OTHER GODS, SPIRITS OF LAND AND SEA

59

Plate 59

The setting sun burnishes the ruins of a classical temple on the island of Rhodes. According to legend the island was the domain of the sun god, Helios; he was able to discern its coming from the sea and he claimed it before the other gods knew of its existence. Rhodos, the nymph of the island (in some traditions the daughter of Aphrodite) became the sun god's consort and she bore him seven sons. The island held an annual festival in honour of Helios and a great festival every fourth year.

60

Plate 60

The sun god depicted on a Greek krater. A team of four winged horses drew his chariot across the sky; when it had crossed the heavens it sank into the western sea, and rose again in the east to bring the returning day. (During the annual festival on Rhodes a team of four horses was sacrificed by being thrown into the sea). Helios was later confused with Apollo—probably because of Apollo's other name which was Phoebus (the bright). But Helios was the original sun god of the Greeks, identified by them as the spirit of a natural phenomenon. For that reason he enjoyed no particular veneration and there was no cult of Helios on the Greek mainland. However he was acknowledged as one who saw and heard everything, and in the *Iliad* Agamamnon calls upon him to witness the oath he takes before the duel of Paris and Menelaus.

61

Plate 61

Selene, the goddess of the moon. Like Helios, she was to be confused in later legends with other deities. Some traditions described her as the sister of the sun god, and appropriately she was most often confused with Artemis the sister of Apollo. Unlike Helios, she had no cult of her own, though evidence suggests that there was something like a moon cult in Crete in very early times. Despite this the Greeks shared with their contemporaries the superstitions about the moon and its influence on organic and erotic life; everything prospered and increased when the moon waxed—the opposite happened when the moon waned. Magic was practised in the light of the rising moon, and the full moon was the time when physical passion would be most intense. The illustration shown here is a detail from a Greek krater and shows Selene on her horse. The moon is in the descendent and goddess and mount are beginning to sink from sight.

62

Plate 62

Asklepios, the god of healing and medicine. That is according to Hesiod—to Homer he was a mortal who was taught the art of healing by Chiron the centaur. Hesiod made him the son of Apollo by the nymph, Coronis, who proved faithless to her divine lover; he complained to his sister Artemis, who killed the nymph with arrows. Then, while watching her funeral pyre burn, Apollo was filled with remorse and he snatched the unborn child of Coronis from the flames. The child was Asklepios and Apollo entrusted him to the care of Chiron. The versions of Homer and Hesiod agree at least on the point that it was from Chiron that he learned the art of healing. Asklepios sometimes incurred the wrath of Zeus and his brother Hades; his skill as a healer could deprive Zeus of revenge by bringing his victim back to life, and deprive Hades' kingdom of inhabitants simply by ensuring that they did not die. He is shown here with his staff and his serpent emblem which signified renewal.

63

Plate 63

The theatre at Epidauros, the Greek city which owed its fame to Asklepios—the centre of his cult was here. Patients would visit the temple and sleep there; a cure would sometimes be communicated through dreams, sometimes be effected during sleep. Snakes were kept in the temple and regarded as sacred, the snake being the god's emblem, and when new cult centres were founded young serpents were taken there from Epidauros. (The small yellow snakes to be seen in the region today, harmless creatures, are very likely those described by the ancient Greek traveller Pausanias). The theatre dates from the fourth century BC and is one of the most perfect of its kind. It is in regular use today.

64

65

66

Plate 64

The great god Pan depicted in bronze by an
Etruscan sculptor of the fourth century BC. A very
ancient god indeed, his cult was in Arcadia
where Mount Maenalus was sacred to him. A
herdsman's god, he came to be associated
with goats which were the principal livestock
of that part of Greece. In Homer he is made the son
of Hermes who was an Olympian and also,
originally, a god of Arcadia. The cult of Pan
reached beyond his native pastures and by the fifth
century BC he had a cave shrine on the Acropolis. He
was reputed to be the cause of sudden and
groundless fear—panic fear—that could overcome
people in desolate, lonely places, and his
principal diversion, sex, was the natural outcome
of his connection with the fertility of flocks. Though
a minor god in classical Greece, Pan enjoyed a
healthy respect. It was from him that Apollo learned
the art of prophecy.

Plate 65

An Etruscan terracotta relief from Cerveteri
showing a satyr dancing with a maenad.
Satyrs were originally shown with some animal-like
features, those of a horse or a goat, and were
variously called the brothers of the nymphs or the
spirits of the wild countryside. They were
associated with both Dionysus and Pan and in later
Greek art often depicted as the familiars of
Dionysus in his character of god of wine. As the
familiars of Pan they often wore horns and walked
on hoofs and this association, particularly, was
the one that gave them in later centuries
their identification as the male symbols of sexuality.
The satyr shown here seems little more than a
frisky young man; but in Roman art that is how he
frequently appears.

Plate 66

A Lycian sarcophagus of the fourth century BC,
showing two centaurs in combat on the front panel.
These strange creatures were originally depicted
as horses with the head of a man. The later,
more familiar idea of a creature half man
and half horse is seen here. They are very old
in Greek legend, much older than Homer and they
appear in both of his epics. In mythology, the
centaurs were begotten by Ixion, who abused the
hospitality of Zeus by casting lustful eyes on Hera.
Zeus divined his intentions and fashioned a false
Hera from a cloud. Ixion, too drunk to notice
anything wrong, seduced the cloud woman,
Nephele, and was then bound by Zeus in
punishment to a fiery wheel which rolled across
the sky eternally, while Nephele descended to earth
and gave birth to a son, Centaurus. This son
mated with the mares of Mount Pelion
and thus sired the race of centaurs. Generally
they were wild, lustful, and strongly attracted to
wine. The exception was the wise and kind
medicine-man Chiron, who differed from the others
being of divine origin.

Plate 67 and 68

Eros was the god of love in Greek mythology, the son of Aphrodite by either Ares or Hermes (there are differing traditions). Homer never mentions Eros as a god, simply referring to *eros* as the force that impels lovers to one another—and makes wise men speak in the language of fools. Hesiod on the other hand believed him to be one of the oldest and most powerful gods, since neither men nor the gods themselves were proof against him. As the personification of physical love he had a large following among the Greeks and he was celebrated annually in a number of festivals. The one in Athens was held in the Spring and phallic symbols have been found in the ruins of his sanctuary. In Greek art he was originally shown as a young man carrying his bow and walking over flowers and plants, as in the gold-painted lekythos. By the Hellenistic period he had become the more familiar baby-like figure, often asleep, as in the marble statue from Paphos.

67

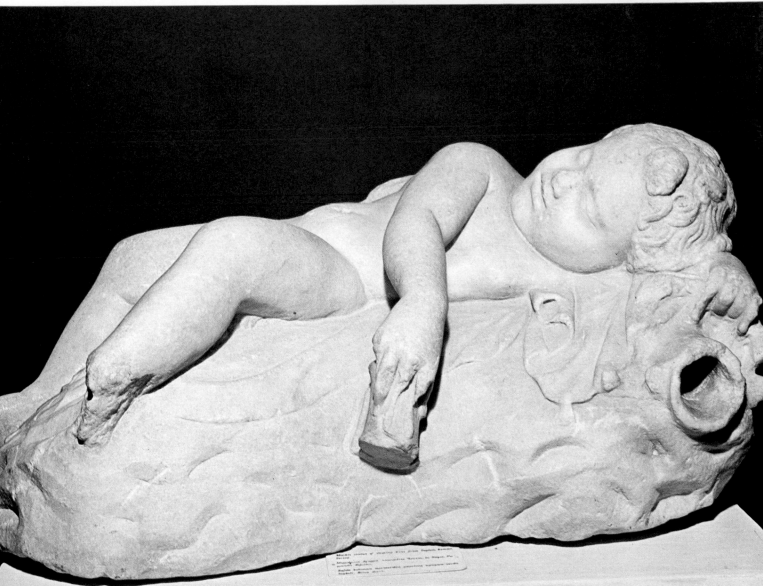

68

69

70

Plate 69

Chiron the centaur with the young Achilles. Chiron played the part of mentor and guardian to Achilles, Jason, Heracles and many other Greek heroes. He was possibly in origin a priest-king of the horse breeders of Thessaly, one to whom they ascribed all wisdom. It was inevitable that his stature increased as the tradition extended down the centuries. Some myths describe him as the king of the centaurs; others say that he was the son of Cronus and therefore immortal. His immortality was to prove no boon; Heracles, while performing his Fourth Labour, accidentally wounded Chiron in the knee—and Heracles used arrows dipped in the poison of Hydra. The wound would have been fatal to a mortal but for Chiron it was infinitely worse, since he would have to endure eternal pain. At length the cruel impasse was overcome; Zeus allowed Chiron to surrender his immortality to Prometheus, and die in peace. Wall painting from Herculaneum.

Plate 70

A view of the Greek countryside with a glimpse of Delphi in the distance. The Greeks acknowledged the spirits of nature in many different ways and the most familiar to us are perhaps the nymphs. Usually believed to be young and beautiful, they were benevolent to mankind as a rule but were not to be trifled with. They punished unresponsive lovers and sometimes stole young men for themselves; they were very like the fairies of later days. There was an infinite variety of them; those of the forests and groves were Dryads, those of meadows Leimoniads, those of mountains Orestiads. There were also the water nymphs; Naiads, Potameids, Creneids and Hydriads. In contrast to the gods the nymphs were mortal, though they were blessed, according to Hesiod, with very long lives.

Plate 71

A Harpy carrying off a child. The Harpies (the name is from a Greek word meaning 'snatchers') were, according to Homer and Hesiod, the personification of violent winds—strong enough to snatch people away. They were usually depicted as birds with the faces of women, and in mythology they are described as the daughters of Thaumas and Electra (daughter of Oceanus—not the sister of Orestes). They make a notable appearance in the story of the Argonauts: when the voyagers reached Salmydessus they found the king, Phineus, in great distress because the Harpies continually plagued him. He had the gift of prophecy, and had earned the wrath of Zeus for using his gift too accurately. The Harpies snatched the food from his table and defiled what they couldn't carry away. The Argonauts rid Phineus of the Harpies, and in turn he gave them valuable advice about the voyage. The relief shown here is in the British Museum and comes from a tomb of the fifth century BC found at Xanthos in Asia Minor.

V
THE STUFF OF TRAGEDY

72

Plate 72

Orpheus and the beasts as depicted on a mosaic from Tarsus of the third
century AD. Orpheus is one of the most celebrated figures in Greek mythology—
and one of the most difficult to identify. According to the myths surrounding
him he was the son of the Muse Calliope, and a musician of such power and
sweetness that the wild creatures would gather to listen to him. He sailed with the
Argonauts, and his wife was the dryad Eurydice who, fleeing from the
attentions of Aristaeus, trod on a serpent and died from its bite. Orpheus went
down to Hades and persuaded him to release her; but the lord of the shades
made the condition that Orpheus must believe that Eurydice followed him to
earth—and not look back. But in his agony of uncertainty that Eurydice
was really following him Orpheus did look back, and saw her slip away from him
for ever.

Plate 73

The Lion Gate, the entrance to the citadel of
Mycenae. Agamemnon was king of Mycenae and
the leader of the Achaean armies that went to Troy
to avenge the stealing of Helen, the most beautiful
of all women and the wife of Menelaus, the king of
Sparta. The brothers and their Achaean allies
were eventually victorious—but the war had
dragged on for ten years. Agamemnon,
who may well have been an historic personage,
might have ridden under the Lion Gate in
the chariot that brought him home, apparently
in triumph. Also in the chariot would have been
Cassandra, the princess of Troy he claimed as part of
his spoils. But there had been another princess—
Agamemnon's daughter Iphigenia, and he had
used her as a sacrifice when the Achaen fleet was
held up at Aulis by contrary winds. He tricked his
wife Clytemnestra into bringing the girl to
Aulis, saying that she was to become the
wife of Achilles. Clytemnestra had been waiting ten
years for the king to return. . . .

73

Plate 74

. . . and in her husband's absence she took a lover,
Aegisthus, and waited for the day when she could be
revenged on Agamemnon. When he returned
from Troy she gave him a welcome befitting a
warrior king; but then murdered both him
and Cassandra when they entered the palace.
This is one of the strange beehive tombs of Mycenae,
which were built into the side of the hill and given
their shape by the use of the corbeled vault. This
is variously called 'the Treasury of Atreus' and
'the Tomb of Clytemnestra' but the actual
use to which the building was put cannot
be determined. If it was indeed a tomb for
Clytemnestra its strangeness is well suited to
the extraordinary woman the Greek tragedians
put into their plays. She is a tremendous figure in
the *Agamemnon* of Aeschylus; and also appears in the
sequel, *The Liberation Bearers*.

74

Plate 75

A fifth-century terracotta showing Electra and
Orestes at the tomb of Agamemnon. The
great tragic cycle which begins with the
sacrifice of Iphigenia rolls on relentlessly. The
most famous dramatic version of the next stage of
events is probably the *Electra* of Sophocles but
the scene shown here, moving though it is, is not
used by that master. It occurs in the *Electra* of
Euripides and *The Libation Bearers* of Aeschylus, and
deals with the encounter of brother and sister at
their father's tomb. In the play by Aeschylus,
Orestes has been in exile since the murder of his
father. He returns with his friend Pylades
and, going at once to his father's tomb,
dedicates on it a lock of his hair. The two
withdraw upon the approach of Electra and her
attendants, who have been sent to pour libations on
the tomb by their guilty mother Clytemnestra
who has been troubled by ominous dreams. Electra
recognizes the lock of hair—exactly like her own
—and brother and sister are reunited.

75

76

77

Plate 76

Orestes avenges the death of his father, Agamemnon. Detail from an amphora in the British Museum. After the encounter at the tomb, Orestes and Pylades proceed to the palace in disguise and tell Clytemnestra that Orestes her son is dead. Exultant, the queen sends for her lover Aegisthus, believing that there can be no threat now to their happiness and safety. When Aegisthus arrives Orestes kills him in front of the Queen. She pleads for her life, and Orestes falters; but he has been commanded by Apollo and drags his mother inside the palace and murders her too.

Plate 77

Cadmus, the brother of Europa and the founder of Thebes. The Delphic oracle told him to follow a cow and found a city where the creature first lay down. This he did, then Athene instructed him to sow the teeth of the dragon he had just killed, and from them grew warriors fully armed. Cadmus provoked these to fight each other by throwing a stone amongst them, and the five best fighters who survived became the ancestors of the noble families of Thebes.

Plate 78

The meeting with the Sphinx, an incident in the tragic life of Oedipus, who became king of Thebes. His father Laius had brought a curse on his family and he was warned by Apollo that his own son would kill him. This was Oedipus, and Laius drove a spike through the baby's feet and left him to die on Mount Cithaeron. A shepherd found him and took him to Polybus and Merope, king and queen of Corinth, who brought him up as their son. Later, upset by taunts that he was no true son of Polybus, Oedipus enquired of the Delphic oracle concerning his true parentage. The oracle only told him that he would bring destruction on his father and marry his own mother, and the horrified Oedipus, loving Polybus and Merope as the only parents he knew, fled from Corinth to avoid doing them harm. On his journey he came to a place where three roads met, and there encountered a man in a chariot who ordered him to get out of his way. A fight ensued and Oedipus killed the man in the chariot who was Laius, his real father. Oedipus went on, and defeated the Sphinx that plagued the city of Thebes, and as a result he was welcomed as a hero. He was offered the hand of Jocasta, the widowed queen, and the throne—the oracle was fulfilled. By his wife-mother, Oedipus became the father of two sons and two daughters, and all went well until, in a time of famine and disease, the oracle was to wreak havoc with him again; the city would know peace, it said, when the unknown murderer of Laius was discovered and cast out. Oedipus sets out to find the truth, and when he does it is too awful to bear; Jocasta hangs herself and Oedipus puts out his eyes. He leaves the city, a blinded exile, attended by his daughter Antigone.

VI
THE HEROES

79

Plate 79

Heracles was the hero of heroes. No one else has left such an impression of
undefeatable strength and fearlessness and it is possible that the character
was based on an ancient hero of Argos who actually lived. His character suggests
that he was much older than the others, like Theseus and Jason; his adventures
depend entirely on his brute strength while the other heroes display a certain wit
and intelligence in the performance of their exploits. Heracles was inclined to
force even when dealing with the gods, as this incident shows. He had
gone to Delphi seeking to be rid of evil dreams after his murder of Iphitus;
the Pythoness had refused to counsel such as he, whereupon he seized the tripod
and smashed the votive offerings in the shrine. When Apollo, wrathful at
such desecration, appeared on the scene Heracles fought him and they
were eventually separated by their father Zeus. The Greeks usually depicted
Heracles as a trim, often handsome man, in contrast to the muscle-bound
heavyweight the Romans made of him.

Plate 80

Heracles was the son of Zeus, who lay with Alcmena in the guise of her absent husband Amphitryon, making the night last three times as long to ensure his begetting. Hera, jealous again at Zeus' coupling with a mortal woman, afflicted Heracles with madness, and the famous Labours were a penalty for the crimes committed during this time. He had to serve Eurystheus, king of Tiryns, for twelve years and perform whatever Labours the king imposed. The First Labour is shown on this Attic vase painting, where Heracles kills the lion that was ravaging Nemea. He skinned the lion with its own claws and thereafter wore the pelt as a cloak.

Plate 81

Heracles and the Hind of Ceryneia. Another one of his Labours was the catching of this creature, a dappled deer with hooves of brass and golden horns (the horns suggest that it may in fact have been a stag) sacred to the goddess Artemis. Four such hinds were harnessed to the chariot of Artemis; the fifth was the one Heracles pursued, the last of the original herd. He hunted her for one whole year and ran her down, exhausted, near the river Ladon. This detail from an Attic vase painting shows Heracles wearing his lion-skin cloak. He is watched by Athene and Artemis, the latter on the right carrying her huntress's bow.

80

81

82

Plate 82

Tiryns, the city most associated with the myths of Heracles, was a very ancient one and possibly existed as long ago as 2,500 BC. The ruins can be seen in the plain of Argos, to the south of Mycenae, and their most famous feature is the incredible walls built of huge roughly-hewn blocks which in some places are more than twenty-five feet thick. Like nearby Mycenae, Tiryns stood on a hill and was a strong fortress; it survived as an inhabited city until it was destroyed by the city of Argos in the early fourth century BC.

Plate 83

Heracles carries the Erymanthian boar back alive. A bronze figure now in the Delphi museum. It was while engaged on this Labour that Heracles accidentally wounded Chiron the centaur. On his way to Mount Erymanthus he was entertained by the centaur Pholus, who possessed a jar of wine given him by Dionysus. When the jar was opened the other centaurs smelled the wine and attacked the cave where Pholus and Heracles were enjoying a meal. Chiron, hearing the noise of the fight, went to see what the trouble was and it was then that an arrow of Heracles' wounded him in the knee.

Heracles eventually caught the boar. It was hidden in a thicket and he shouted until it emerged; then he drove it up the hillside toward a deep snowdrift. The speed of the beast was thus reduced and he was able to catch up with it. He bound it with chains and carried it on his shoulders to king Eurystheus, who was so terrified by the struggling, snarling creature that he jumped into a bronze jar to hide from it.

83

Plate 84

The Stymphalian birds were sacred to Ares. They were man-eaters and had claws and wings of brass and their excrement was poisonous to the crops. They lived in the Stymphalian marsh and the people of the neighbouring countryside went in terror of them; sometimes in flight they would shed their brazen feathers from a great height which were as dangerous as arrows. Heracles paused by the marsh and could devise no way of dealing with the plague; he could not walk in the soft mud and he could not use a boat among the thick reeds. The goddess Athene came to his aid in this Labour; on her advice he took a brass rattle and climbed on to a spur of Mount Cyllene. He made a mighty noise, and continued with such persistence that the birds took fright and flew up from the marsh. He was then able to kill many of them with arrows. He repeated this trick and so decimated the flock that the remainder, terrified, flew off to the east and left the region in peace. Detail from a fifth-century amphora.

84

Plate 85

As a penalty for desecrating the shrine at Delphi, Heracles had to serve as a slave for one year. His owner was Omphale, the queen of Lydia, and one of the services he performed for her was the capture of two clever thieves, the Cercopes. He tied their feet and hung them head downward from a pole; then he swung them across his shoulders and carried them off to justice. He had gone a little way when he noticed that his captives were whispering to each other— soon they were chuckling. Their laughter continued and by paying attention to their whispers Heracles realized that they were laughing at him. He wore only his lion-skin cloak, which reached no farther down than his waist; his buttocks and thighs were constantly exposed to the sun. The Cercopes were exchanging wisecracks about 'old black-bottom' their captor. In the end he started laughing himself, and was persuaded to let them go. A relief of the sixth century BC from Selinunte.

85

86

87

Plate 86

Heracles and the centaur Nessus. The hero won the hand of Deianira, princess of Calydon, and on the way to Trachis they found the river Euenus in flood. Heracles could not breast the flood and carry Deianira as well, so he agreed that the centaur Nessus should ferry the princess across. No sooner was Deianira mounted on the centaur's back than Nessus galloped away with her. An arrow from Heracles stopped his flight, and while he lay dying Nessus told Deianira to keep some of his blood, and smear it on her husband's clothes to prevent him being unfaithful to her; and this Deianira did. She remembered the centaur's advice when Heracles announced his intention of marrying another woman, and sent him a robe anointed with the blood of Nessus. It was fatal; the arrows of Heracles were poisoned with the blood of the Hydra—Nessus knew that perfectly well and his blood was poisoned too. Heracles, to end his agony, had a funeral pyre prepared. He was carried to it, and upon his death took his place with his father Zeus on Olympus.

Plate 87

One adventure of Heracles was oddly confused with those of another hero, Theseus, and it is generally believed that some of the former's deeds were unsuccessfully grafted on to those of the latter to increase his heroic status. In this fragment from Delphi Theseus is shown defeating the Amazon queen; the Amazons had invaded Attica when Theseus abducted one of them, Antiope. Heracles, in his adventure, was to capture the girdle of Hippolyta, queen of the Amazons, because the daughter of Eurystheus wanted it. He succeeded in getting it, and there are various accounts of how this was done. One version says that he killed her for it; but the Amazon wife of Theseus was called Hippolyta—she might have been another Amazon queen but the appearance of her name in both adventures suggests that one adventure has not very successfully been made into two.

Plate 88

Heracles about to embark on another adventure, and one in which he played a minor part. This painting on a fifth-century krater shows the Argonauts gathering for their voyage, under the command of Jason, to capture the Golden Fleece. Jason was the son of Aeson, king of Iolcos. Aeson's kingdom was usurped by his half-brother Pelias, and Jason was sent for safety to the care of Chiron the centaur. As a man he returned to Pelias' court; the king sent him on the quest for the Golden Fleece, hoping to be rid of the threat to his uneasy throne. Jason built the *Argo* and fifty Greek heroes, including Heracles and Orpheus, sailed with him to Colchis at the eastern shore of the Black Sea. The goddess Athene is standing on the left, while Jason converses with Heracles who is as usual naked except for his lion skin. Jason succeeded in his quest, largely because of the help given him by the witch-queen of Colchis, Medea, who fell in love with him.

89

Plate 89

Theseus was a hero of Athens, and that city claimed him as the true founder of the state. One of the early kings, Aegeus, stopped at the city of Troezen on his way back from Delphi, and made love to the princess Aethra. (Some versions have it that she was also loved by Poseidon, and that Theseus was in fact the son of a god. He enjoyed the sea-god's protection during his adventures.) When Aegeus returned to Athens, he left his sword and his sandals concealed under a heavy rock; he told Aethra that if she bore a son, and he could succeed in lifting the rock and recover the tokens—then Aegeus would acknowledge him as his heir. Theseus was only sixteen when he succeeded in this task; he could have sailed to Athens there and then but he preferred to go by land, crossing the dangerous Isthmus road. That was the beginning of his exploits. This Roman relief of the late first century AD shows him lifting the rock—and looking rather more than sixteen years old. The relief is now in the British Museum.

90

Plate 90

The interior of a painted kylix from Vulci showing the exploits of Theseus. The centre is occupied by the most famous exploit of all—the encounter with the Minotaur; directly above it he can be seen wrestling with Kerkyon, who waylaid travellers near Eleusis and challenged them to wrestle with him. Through his brute strength he usually won; but Theseus brought skill to the combat and managed to kill him. Reading clockwise, the next scene shows him killing Procrustes, who had a nasty habit of trimming—or stretching—his guests to fit his bed. Next is the evil Sinis, whose victims were hurled to their death on trees which he bent down to the ground for the purpose. Third is the great bull that ravaged the plain of Marathon, and then Sciron the bandit who threw his victims into the sea. The pictures end with Theseus defeating the monstrous sow bred by Phaea of Crommyon, which so terrorised the people that they dared not venture into their fields. At length Theseus reached Athens, only to meet another, more subtle, danger. His father Aegeus had in the meantime married the witch-queen Medea, whom Jason had brought back from Colchis and then spurned. She nearly succeeded in poisoning Theseus; but Aegeus recognized the sword that Theseus carried and dashed the cup from his hand. So Theseus took his rightful place in Athens, and it wasn't long before he set out on the greatest adventure of all.

Plate 91

An Attic amphora of the fifth century BC, showing the killing of the Minotaur in realistic detail. King Aegeus was obliged to send seven youths and seven maidens each year to Crete, a penalty for the death, in Athens, of Androgeos the son of the Cretan king, Minos. None of them ever returned; upon reaching his kingdom Minos put them in the Labyrinth—a maze from which it was impossible to escape—to be devoured by the Minotaur. The Minotaur was the offspring of the queen, Pasiphae, who conceived an unnatural passion for a fine bull that emerged from the sea. The result of this union was a creature half man and half bull, and the Labyrinth was constructed by Daedalus to hide it in.

Theseus volunteered to go as one of the seven youths. When the ship arrived in Crete the king's daughter Ariadne saw him and fell in love with him, and it was she who conceived the idea of using a ball of thread, given her by Daedalus, to show Theseus the way in and out of the Labyrinth. The ball of thread unwound itself, showing him the way to the Minotaur's lair. He killed the monster, and then followed the thread to escape from the maze. He and his companions fled from Crete, taking Ariadne with them, and stopped at Naxos on the way home. Some traditions say that while on Naxos the hero was visited by Dionysus in a dream; the god demanded Ariadne for himself. Whatever the reason for it, Theseus did abandon Ariadne, who lay weeping on the shore until Dionysus, returning to Greece, reached the island and consoled her with his love.

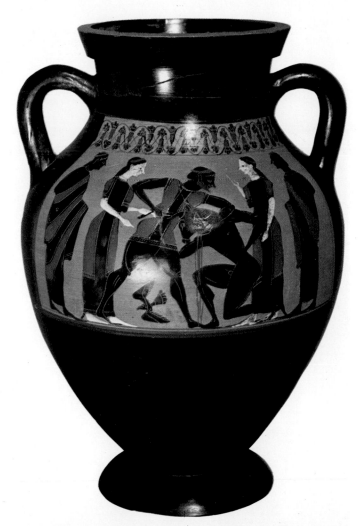

91

Plate 92

Perseus slaying the Gorgon. A sixth-century relief from Selinunte. This hero was, like Heracles, a son of Zeus; his mother was Danae, daughter of Acrisius who really wanted a son. The oracle told him that he would have no heir—but to beware of his daughter's son. He promptly imprisoned her in an underground chamber; but it was too late —she had been seen by Zeus and the god visited her as a shower of gold which poured into her lap. Danae seems to have had a fatal fascination; her father cast her adrift in a chest on the sea as soon as her son was born, and it drifted to the island of Seriphus. The king of Seriphus immediately fell in love with her, and decided to get rid of her son. Perseus was sent to get the Gorgon's head, and a glance from the Gorgon could turn any man to stone. However he was fortunate in his allies: with winged sandals from Hermes he could fly, with a cap from Hades he could become invisible, and in some versions Athene leant him her shield to use as a mirror and thus avoid the Gorgon's glance. Athene is seen here beside the hero, and in the Gorgon's lap is Pegasus. (The magic horse was the child of the Gorgon by Poseidon, and in this relief is, strangely, shown without the wings which were his most famous feature).

92

VII
ILIAD & ODYSSEY

93

Plate 93

It is not known for certain when it was that Homer wrote, though the scant evidence that exists suggests that it was some time in the eighth century BC. His life is also unknown to us; the few hints that can be gleaned from the text of the *Iliad* have led to the assumption that he was a Greek of Ionia but there is nothing positive. This has led to doubt that there ever was a tragic poet who composed two great epics, that what we know as the *Iliad* and the *Odyssey* were simply collections of heroic lays strung together over a period of time. Most scholars now dismiss that theory; the poems bear the evidence of a single creator in their unity of style and their consistency of character. They could not have simply evolved.

The *Iliad* concerns the war between Troy and the Achaens (Homer never calls them Greeks) over the abduction of Helen by the Trojan prince, Paris. The *Odyssey* is the long, adventurous journey home of the king of Ithaca, Odysseus, who went to the war unwillingly but proved as valint as—and much cleverer than—Achilles, Ajax, Diomedes, Menelaus, Agememnon and the rest. The illustration, from a Lucanian krater, shows Odysseus and Diomedes in one of the lesser known incidents; they make a raid by night on the Trojan lines and stumble on Dolon, a Trojan who was attempting to spy on the Achaean camp. Dolon proves unequal to the ordeal of their threats and gives them valuable information. But they murder him anyway.

Plate 94

Menelaus and Hector, the Trojan prince, in combat. The dead man is the Trojan, Euphorbus, and this painted plate from Rhodes is known as the Euphorbus plate. Patroclus led the attack on Troy while Achilles was sulking in his tent, and Euphorbus gave him his first wound; Hector finished him off. Menelaus killed Euphorbus—but did not long try conclusions with the great Hector. However, he and Ajax returned for the body of Patroclus and bore it back to the Achaean camp. It was this that roused Achilles from his sulks; he loved Patroclus, and the news that he was killed roused Achilles to fury. He meant to have Hector's life in return.

Plate 95

Hector and Achilles face to face. Achilles mounted a furious attack on the Trojans that drove them back into the city. Hector met him at the Scaean Gate and the two champions knew that one of them must fall. It was Hector. To the horror of the Trojans watching from the walls, Achilles despoiled the corpse by tying it to the back of his chariot and dragging it through the dust back to his camp. There he sacrificed twelve Trojan prisoners on the funeral pyre of Patroclus; but he intended that Hector's body should be thrown to the dogs. In the meantime he went on despoiling it, but Apollo was moved to compassion and preserved his body from damage. On the twelfth day the gods, outraged by Achilles' vile behaviour, decided that Hector's body should be restored to his father Priam for decent burial. The Messenger goddess Iris went to Troy, and inspired Priam to go to the Achaen camp. The old king pleaded with Achilles, and finally yielded his daughter Polyxena as a bride for Achilles as well as Hector's weight in gold. Achilles gave way, and the corpse of the noble Hector was taken back to Troy for burial.

94

96

97

Plate 96

After the wooden Horse. The Achaeans took the city, and no mercy was shown to the Trojans. Cassandra, Priam's daughter, fled to the temple of Athene for sanctuary. She was pursued there by Ajax who dragged her away from the altar; thus he earned the wrath of Athene and the loathing of the other Achaeans for violating a sacred shrine. The painting of this fourth-century lekythos shows Apollo watching the scene. Apollo had fallen in love with Cassandra but she had resisted him; in consequence the god had given her the gift of prophecy—and then made it useless. No one believed her, though she had in fact prophesied the city's doom. Ajax had to yield Cassandra to Agamemnon when the spoils were divided, and she met the same fate as her captor when he returned to Mycenae.

Plate 97

The sack of Troy. Priam, lying on the ground, was killed by Neoptolemus, the son of Achilles. Hecuba, the queen of Troy, fell to the lot of Odysseus, though this fact was lost in the telling of his subsequent adventures. The son of Hector and Andromache, the last of the Trojan royal line, is seen being carried off by the Achaean herald, Talthybius. The child could not be allowed to live, and Talthybius, acting on the orders of Odysseus, hurled him from the walls. Andromache was given to Neoptolemus, and Polyxena was sacrificed on the tomb of Achilles. The beautiful Helen, the apparent cause of the war, was threatened with death by her husband Menelaus but her beauty destroyed his resolve and he took her back to Sparta with him. The Achaeans destroyed the city by fire after plundering it.

Plate 98

On his way home from Troy Odysseus landed on the island of the Cyclops, giant herdsmen who were said to be the sons of Poseidon, and who had only one eye. Odysseus and his companions explored a cave which proved to be the home of one of the Cyclops, Polyphemus, who returned unexpectedly and sealed the exit with a huge rock after his flock of sheep were safely inside. He discovered the men and promptly ate two of them; the next day he ate two more. Odysseus, in the way of epic heroes, just happened to have a full wine-skin with him, which sent Polyphemus into a drunken sleep. Odysseus took a burning brand from the fire in the cave and thrust it into the giant's single eye; Polyphemus in his agony screamed for his brother Cyclops to come and help him. Now Odysseus, asked by Polyphemus who he was, had answered 'I am Noman'. When his brother Cyclops asked Polyphemus what he was screaming about he told them that Noman had blinded him. They went away again, annoyed that he should be raving about something that no man was doing to him; and assuming he was having nightmares.

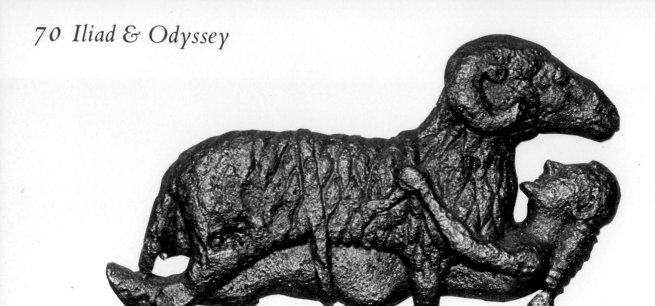

99

100

Plate 99

When the dawn came Polyphemus rolled away the rock that sealed the cave, as his flock had to be let out to pasture; but he sat by the entrance and used his hands to tell him which creatures were leaving the cave. Odysseus tied his men under the bellies of the finest rams and in this way they escaped from the Cyclops. There was no one to tie Odysseus so he chose the biggest ram, the leader of the flock, and simply clung to the fleece. This bronze from Delphi shows him making his escape. With the remainder of his men Odysseus got back to his ship and took his rams on board to provide meat for the crew. Then he stood at the prow and shouted taunts at the blinded giant, who responded by hurling huge rocks at the ship. Not being able to see the ship he failed to destroy it; but he called on his father Poseidon to avenge him. Falling foul of the sea god was unwise, as Odysseus was to discover; a journey back from the Trojan war was to last ten years.

Plate 100

Odysseus and Circe, from a Theban vase of the fourth century. Circe, looking somewhat less than an enchantress, offers a drink to Odysseus, who looks somewhat less than a hero. The events of the Trojan war and the return of Odysseus were favourite subjects among the Greek painters and the quality of the work was, inevitably, of enormous range, and this representation is not one of the best. On the island of Aeaea Odysseus went off to explore, and when he returned to the ship divided his company into two parties to go and investigate the smoke he had seen rising from a clearing. One party found the palace of Circe; she invited them in and gave them food and drink. But the food turned them into pigs. Odysseus, going to their rescue, was warned by the god Hermes, who gave him a magic herb known only to the gods. So Odysseus was immune to Circe's magic, and he forced her to restore his men to their human form. However he was not immune to Circe's personal charms; he dallied with her for a whole year.

Plate 101

An Attic vase painting of the fifth century BC showing Odysseus and the Sirens. When he left the island of Aeaea he was warned by Circe that he would have to sail past the Sirens, who lured the crews of ships to destruction on the rocks by their sweet singing—no one who heard the song could resist following it. (They make an appearance in the epic of the Argonauts also; but on that occasion they could not compete with Orpheus, who outsang them). Odysseus ordered his men to bind him to the mast of the ship, first taking the precaution to block up their ears to prevent them from hearing the songs themselves.
In this way the Sirens were safely eluded. They were half woman and half bird, and their conception may have been an echo of the time when birds were regarded as messengers of death. Some traditions said that the Sirens died if their song was resisted, and one of them can be seen falling dead into the sea.

101

Plate 102

When Odysseus finally reached Ithaca he disguised himself as a beggar on the advice of the goddess Athene. His first encounter was with his old swineherd Eumaeus, who told the stranger of what had befallen in the palace while the king was away on a war from which he had never returned; that the palace was full of suitors despoiling the king's household, and trying to persuade Penelope, the queen, to marry one of them in the hope of gaining the throne. Odysseus continued to the palace, having made himself known to his son Telemachus, and there was only recognized by his old dog Argus who, lying neglected on a dung heap, was able to give him one last, hopeful wag of his tail before dying. Penelope, hearing from the stranger that he knew her husband, treated him as an honoured guest and asked his old nurse, Eurycleia, to bring water and wash the stranger's feet.
The incident is shown here on a Roman relief of the first century AD. Eurycleia recognized Odysseus by an old scar from a wound he had sustained while hunting boar.
Eventually Odysseus made himself known to Penelope; but not until he had killed the suitors and regained his kingdom.

102

ACKNOWLEDGMENTS

The publishers would like to thank the following individuals and organizations for their kind permission to reproduce the pictures in this book:

Page

F H C Birch/Sonia Halliday Photographs — 3, 16, 18, 91, 21, 22 top, 28, 29 top, 31, 33 centre and bottom, 35 bottom, 49, 55 top and centre.

BPC Library — 24–25.

C M Dixon — 17, 20, 22 bottom, 23 (& jacket), 24, 26 top, 27, 29 bottom, 30 top, 38, 39 top, 40 top, 43 centre, 44, 52 bottom, 53, 57, 60 bottom, 62 bottom, 64 top, 70 top, 71 top.

Giraudon (Musé Louvre) — 42 bottom, 55 bottom, 63, 65 top.

Sonia Halliday Photographs — 33 top, 39 bottom, 40 bottom, 41, 46 top, 48 bottom, 51, 54, 60 top, 61 bottom, 65 bottom.

Andre Held/Joseph Ziolo — 29 centre, 32 top, 34 top.

Hirmer Fotoarchiv — 2, 26 bottom, 43 bottom.

Michael Holford — endpapers, 30 bottom, 34 centre and bottom, 36, 37 bottom, 42 top, 43 top, 46 bottom, 48 top and centre, 50 top and centre, 51 top, 56, 58, 59, 61 top, 64 bottom, 66, 67, 68, 69, 70 bottom, 71 bottom.

Roland/Joseph Ziolo — 7, 32 bottom.

Scala — 22 centre, 52 top.

Spectrum — 1, 11, 35 top, 37 top, 38 bottom, 45, 47.